The Wise Ow
DANTES Subject Standardized Test (DSST)

Here's to Your Health

Second Edition

Copyright © 2009 Wise Owl Publications, LLC

All rights reserved. No part of this book shall be reproduced, stored in a retrieval system, or transmitted by any means, electronic, mechanical, photocopying, recording, or otherwise, without written permission from the publisher. No patent liability is assumed with respect to the use of the information contained herein. Although every precaution has been taken in the preparation of this book, the publisher and author assume no responsibility for errors or omissions.

Printed in the United States of America

ISBN-10: 1449590454
ISBN-13: 9781449590451
Library of Congress Control Number: 2009912016

Cover design © Wise Owl Publications, LLC

© 2009 All Rights Reserved.
DSST is a registered trademark of Prometric.
This book is not affiliated with Prometric.

Table of Contents

Introduction 6

Using this guide 7

Part I. Health, wellness, and mind/body connection 8

Responsible health, wellness, and lifestyles 9
- Healthy lifestyle 9
- Maslow's hierarchy of needs 10
- Mental health defined 11

Depression types 11

Psychological disorders 13

Stress management and coping mechanisms 16

Addictive behaviors 18

Part II. Human development and relationships 19

Reproduction 19

Sexuality 28
- Sexual orientation 29
- Alternative sexual behaviors 29
- Sexually deviant behaviors 30

Intimate relationships 31

Communication 31

Stages of attraction and kinds of love 32

Healthy aging 34
- Becoming an adult 34
- Midlife 34
- Elderly 34

Death and bereavement 36
- Euthanasia 36
- Hospice care 36

    Bereavement 36
    What you can do to prepare for the inevitable 37

Part III. Substance use and abuse 38

  Alcohol 40
    Effects of alcohol 40
    Symptoms of alcohol poisoning 42
    Alcohol related health issues 42
    Alcohol related social issues 43
    Alcoholism 43

  Tobacco 45
    The compounds of the cigarette 46
    Smoking and the blood 46
    Other Complications of Tobacco Use 46

  Other drugs 48
    Types of drugs 52

  The Effects of Combining Drugs 54

  Herbal remedies 55

Part IV. Fitness and nutrition 57

  Two types of exercise 58

  Muscles 58

  Obesity 59
    Slimming down 59

  Good nutrition and its effects 61
    Sources of nutrients 61
    The food groups 63
    Vegetarians 67

Part V. Risk factors, disease, and disease prevention 68

  Infectious diseases, including sexually transmitted diseases, prevention and control 68

Necessary components of a disease 68
Infectious stages 69

Immune system response 70
Kinds of immunity 71

Common infectious diseases 71

Common sexually transmitted diseases 75

The major systems of the body 78

Cancer 88
Types of cancer and where they are found 88
Treatment of cancer 89

Diabetes, arthritis, and genetic-related disorders 91
Diabetes 91
Asthma 91
Arthritis 92
Genetic disorders 93

Part VI. Consumer awareness, safety, and environmental concerns 96

Consumer awareness 96

Safety concerns 99

Environmental concerns 101

Practice test 103

Answer key 111

Index 113

INTRODUCTION

Are you going to learn everything about health in this study guide? Absolutely not! But . . . are you going to learn enough to pass the DSST test? Yes! In this book we focus on what you need to know, that is it. The DSST (Dantes Subject Standardized Test) series tests cover what is most commonly taught in a college course. That leaves out a lot of content that might be taught in a formal class. So expect to see some questions that you don't know. But, the goal isn't to get 100 percent right. To do that you would need to take a traditional class and invest lots of time, money, and effort. The goal here is simply to pass. Prepare for this test with this study guide and you will be well on your way to a degree in significantly less time than hitting the books in night school (this is not to say it is any easier to get a degree this way, just more flexible)! This book is written in a format that's easy-to-read, understand, and remember. Health is a fascinating topic, and no matter if you have a test to pass or not this information will make you feel like a more educated person for knowing it. Even if you *think* you know everything there is to know about health, this book will teach you a thing or two!

Using this guide

First, this study guide is not a textbook. It is a study guide that will help you identify the most important (and most heavily tested) topics in the health course. If you feel the need, you can purchase a textbook (it doesn't have to be the latest edition) in order to gain an in-depth look into health. Then, you can follow along with this study guide to help you pull out the exact information you need in order to pass the test. What you do depends on your goal. Are you in it simply for the credits, or do you also enjoy the process of learning? There is no right or wrong answer to this question.

PART I. HEALTH, WELLNESS, AND MIND/BODY CONNECTION

This portion of the material will consist of approximately 20 percent of the exam. Part I will cover:

- Responsible health and wellness
- Definition of mental health
- Psychological disorders
- Stress management and coping
- Addictive behaviors

There are five dimensions to health:

- **Physical health**
    - Susceptibility to physical disease.
    - Physical wellness is determined by senses (sight, sound, hearing, taste, and touch), coordination, and strength.

- **Emotional health**
    - Ability to deal with stress, compromise, conflict, and to have emotionally appropriate responses to external stimuli.

- **Social health**
    - Ability to navigate the social environment (office workers, classroom peers, etc).

- **Intellectual health**
    - Creativity, problem solving skills, and ability to process information.

- **Spiritual health**
    - Ability to understand your purpose in the world and your ability to serve others.

RESPONSIBLE HEALTH, WELLNESS, AND LIFESTYLES

The basic concepts covered in this section are:
- Healthy lifestyle
- Maslow's Hierarchy of Needs
- Mental health defined
- Depression
- Psychological disorders
- Stress management
- Addictive behaviors

HEALTHY LIFESTYLE

Holistic health focuses on the entire health spectrum (physical, psychological, social, intellectual, and spiritual). A healthy lifestyle should focus on a holistic approach. Choosing a healthy lifestyle includes:

- Good diet
- Proper exercise
- Enough sleep
- Preventative care
- No illegal drugs
- No tobacco products
- Alcohol consumption

Empowerment is choosing to focus on controlling what a person has power over. For example, nothing can be done about genetic predisposition; however, exercise and eating regimes can be modified. Empowerment is an important to the concept of wellness.

Maslow's Hierarchy of Needs

Abraham Maslow's philosophy on the **Hierarchy of Needs** is displayed in Figure 1 on the next page. The needs are:

- **Physiological needs**
    - Food, water, shelter, and clothing
    - If these most basic needs are not reasonably fulfilled, then a person does not ascend to the next stage of development.
    - For example, a starving person may not focus on safety until the pangs of hunger have been satiated.
- **Safety**
    - Money, home, and a society that protects against violence
- **Social**
    - Marriage, friendship, sexuality
    - Resolves feelings of loneliness and isolation.
- **Esteem**
    - Esteem for self and others
    - Resolves feelings of worthlessness.
- **Self-actualization**
    - Maslow explains this need as an individual doing what they are "meant" to do.

Maslow referred to those that did reach self-actualization as **Transcenders** and **Theory Z** people. He also opined that they were the happiest, most well adjusted people of all. Striving to be all that you are meant to can increase your satisfaction with your life.

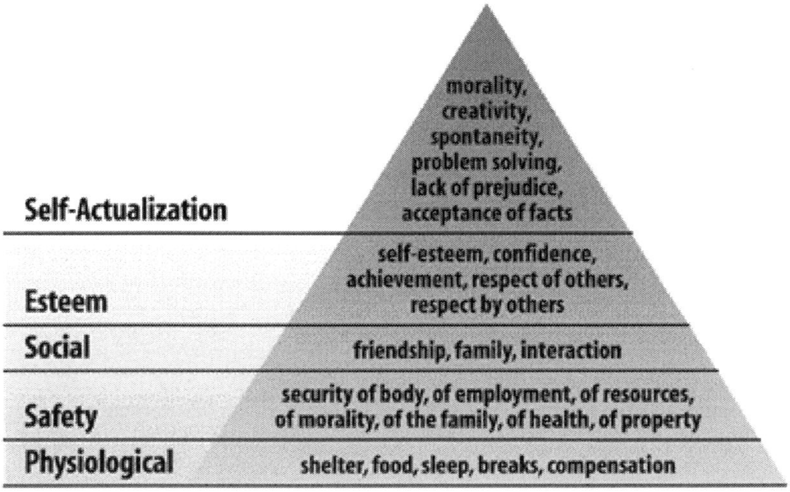

FIGURE 1

Mental health defined

Mentally healthy people are comfortable "in their own skin" and feel confident they can meet the demands of life. This is not to say mentally healthy people don't have negative feelings, because they do (everyone does). However, when mentally healthy people are faced with negative feelings (disappointment, anger, jealousy, or regret) they can a handle the feelings without succumbing to them.

Depression types

Depression is an overwhelming feeling of worthlessness, despair, and sadness that exaggerates reality. It is one of the most common psychological disorders. There are two types of depression, it is important to understand the types because each has a different treatment.

- **Primary depression**
    - Onset for no apparent reason.
    - Primary depression is usually attributed to brain chemistry.

- o The most successful treatment for primary depression is antidepressants.

- **Secondary depression**
    - o Also known as **reactive depression**.
    - o Onset can be clearly identified to a traumatic event (e.g. death, divorce).
    - o The most successful treatment for secondary depression is counseling, and other therapies.

A third kind of depression is called **Season Affective Disorder (SAD)**. SAD is a disorder that is directly related to the amount of sunlight an individual is exposed to. In colder climates (where indoor activity is required) many people suffer from this kind of depression. **Phototherapy** (exposure to fluorescent lights) can help alleviate the symptoms. The symptoms are similar to those of ordinary depression.

Loneliness is not the same as depression. Loneliness is being alone, but desiring human company. Being alone is not synonymous with being lonely. Many individuals seek "alone time" to re-charge their batteries.

PSYCHOLOGICAL DISORDERS

There are several different types of mental disorders; some are less debilitating and more treatable than others. At a minimum you will need to know the types of disorders so you can comfortably pick from them in a multiple-choice test. The main types of disorders are:

- **Anxiety**
    - Disorder that causes physical symptoms such as rapid heartbeat and tenseness.
    - There are several types of anxiety disorders:
        - **Phobia**
            - An irrational fear of something.
            - Some common phobias are **acrophobia** (heights) and **claustrophobia** (closed spaces).
            - A less common, but more debilitating fear is one of open spaces (**agoraphobia**).
        - **Obsessive compulsive disorder (OCD)**
            - Irrational thoughts and associated compulsions to do things over and over again.
        - **Panic**
            - Fear of going crazy and losing control without a compelling reason to do so.
        - **Generalized anxiety disorder**
            - Non-distinct anxiety that lasts for at least a month.
- **Dissociative disorders**
    - Causes a sudden and temporary change in identity or consciousness.

- o **Psychogenic amnesia**
    - Inability to recall a stressful event.
- o **Psychogenic fugue**
    - Sufferer moves to a new place and starts a new identity.

- **Somatoform disorders**
    - o Physical ailment without medical information to support it.
    - o **Hypochondria**
        - Belief of sickness with no medical evidence.
    - o **Conversion disorder**
        - Unexplained loss of body part.

- **Affective disorders**
    - o Inability to express emotion
    - o **Dysthymic**
        - Lasting longer than two years diagnosed by a lack of energy, self-esteem, pessimistic outlook, and the inability to enjoy other people.
    - o **Depressive disorders**
        - More extreme than the dysthymic, and are typically accompanied by a loss of appetite, and weight, with an exaggerated hopeless view of reality.
    - o **Bipolar disorder**
        - Formerly known as manic depressant.
        - All feelings cyclical and to extremes (happiness and depression).

- **Schizophrenic disorders**
    - Affects verbal behavior and perceptions of reality
    - Symptoms include hallucinations, delusions of grandeur, persecution, and exhibit slow or very quick movement.
    - **Disorganized types**
        - Delusions, hallucinations, and an exaggerated social impairment.
    - **Catatonic types**
        - May hold a single position for hours and not respond to speech.
    - **Paranoid types**
        - Typically suffer from delusions of being persecuted that are complex and often have hallucinations to support their altered reality.

Hans Selye, considered the father of stress theory, defined stress as the "nonspecific response of the body to any demand made on it". Stress can emit an emotional and/or a physiological response. The stimulus causing the stress is called the **stressor**. Common stressors are; employment, marriage, parenting, and school.

Not all stress is bad. The body is stressed during exercise or the desire to perform well on a test. Good stress is called **eustress**. Of course, when we talk or think about stress we usually mean the bad stress (**distress**). If stress is not handled appropriately, then the body is more susceptible to ailments such as; hypertension, stroke, heart disease, kidney disease, depression, alcoholism, gastrointestinal disorders (ulcers, IBS), migraines, allergies, asthma, hay fever, insomnia, impotence, and menstrual irregularities.

Selye's theory on stress is called the General Adaption Syndrome (GAS). GAS has three stages:

- **Alarm reaction**
    - When the body encounters an initial stressor and humans exhibit the fight or flight response.
    - The fight or flight response is caused by the surge of adrenaline from **cortisol** (a hormone) secretion into the bloodstream.
    - Physical reactions such as; heart rate increase, throat drying, palms sweating, dizziness, lightheadedness, and a nauseous feeling are common in the alarm reaction stage.
    - Depending on the choice, the body will begin to react (fight or flight).
- **Stage of resistance**
    - The body cannot keep the levels of adrenaline and energy at the reaction stage.

- o The body will begin to try to reach homeostasis after the threat has passed.

- **Stage of exhaustion**
    - o Stressed body will be tired.
    - o The adrenaline surge and return to homeostasis takes a lot of energy from your body.
    - o Depending on the stressor the body may have a weakened immune system, or an overwhelming need for rest to recuperate.

Friedman and Rosenman opined a theory that people either had Type A or Type B personalities. The authors believe that slowing down is significant factor to reduce stress levels and their associated diseases. Type A people typically are more stressed than Type B people. Type A people should focus on; physically slowing down, listening without interruption or finishing sentences, offer appreciation, tone down cynicism, be realistic, accept things that they cannot change, and live each day well.

ADDICTIVE BEHAVIORS

Typical addictions today are; drugs, shopping, eating, gambling, television, video games, work, alcohol, and sex.

Regardless of an addiction, the process is the same. There are three stages of forming an addiction:

- **Exposure**
    - A person is exposed to an activity or drug that they find stimulating in some way.

- **Compulsion**
    - A person invests more time and resources into the addictive activity.
    - Everyday life becomes much less important than the addictive activity.

- **Loss of control**
    - Behavior worsens despite the consequences.
    - The person may begin to come up with excuses so they do not have to give up their behavior.

PART II. HUMAN DEVELOPMENT AND RELATIONSHIPS

This portion of the material will consist of approximately 20 percent of the exam. Part II will cover:

- Reproduction
- Sexuality
- Intimate relationships
- Healthy aging
- Death and bereavement

REPRODUCTION

Reproduction includes birth control methods, fertility, pregnancy symptoms, and birth.

BIRTH CONTROL

- **Birth control** attempts to stop a birth from happening, while contraception is just a small part of the larger subject of birth control.
    - In **contraception,** the goal is to stop an egg from being fertilized.
- **Barrier methods** (a form of contraception) are methods of which a part of the body is covered (forming a barrier) by a foreign object to prevent fertilization of an ovum.
    - Examples of the barrier methods are condoms, cervical cones, and diaphragms.
    - Typically, these methods also are used for people that want to avoid sexually transmitted diseases (however nothing except abstinence will protect 100%).

- Withdrawal
    - The withdrawal method (**coitus interruptus**) is not an effective method of contraception. The fluid before ejaculation typically has viable sperm in it capable of egg fertilization.
- Spermicidal fluid
    - Spermicides are typically used in conjunction with another form of protection.
- Periodic abstinence
    - Three variations; calendar, basal body temperature, and the Billings cervical mucus method.
    - All methods are based on abstaining from sex during times of peak fertility for natural planning purposes.
- Contraceptive pill ("the pill")
    - The oral contraceptive pill prevents ovulation and implantation.
    - The pill is associated with certain health risks.
- Contraceptive drugs
    - Other contraceptive drugs are; **Depo-Provera** (an injection that lasts three months) and subdermal implants (slow release hormones implanted under the skin).
- Sterilization
    - On the extreme end of the contraception spectrum is **sterilization**. For men that means a vasectomy, and for women a hysterectomy (uterus removal) or getting their tubes tied.

- Intrauterine device
    - This device makes the uterus an unsuitable environment for the fertilized egg to implant and the egg is consequently expelled from the body.

ABORTION

- With the controversial decision of Roe vs. Wade, abortion became legal in 1973.
- In early pregnancy the menstrual extraction (aka menstrual induction, menstrual regulation, preemptive abortion) is typically done with a local anesthetic.
    - Suction is applied to the endometrial (uterus lining) tissue.
- If the pregnancy has progressed beyond a few weeks, then vacuum aspiration may be necessary (this is the most common), it is similar to menstrual extraction with the exception that dilation may be required.
- If the pregnancy has progressed to the second trimester, a dilation and evacuation procedure is performed. A hypertonic saline (salt) solution can be injected into the amniotic sac, which will expel the uterine contents. Or, hormones are injected causing contractions to become strong enough to expel the contents.
- For nearly all types of abortions (and some miscarriages) a D&C is necessary. A D&C (Dilation and Curettage) is performed under general anesthesia by dilating the cervix and scraping the uterine walls.

- Factors that can negatively affect fertilization are:
  - Acid level in the vagina
  - Cervical mucus is thick throughout most of the female menstrual cycle
  - In comparison to the surface of the cervix the opening is very small
  - Half of the sperm that do make it to the fallopian tubes travel up the wrong one.
- Factors in favor of fertility are:
  - Sperm is deposited near the cervix
  - Men make a strong alkaline solution for the sperm that can help offset the acidity in the vaginal secretions
  - Sperms move quickly and can live in the fallopian tubes for days
  - When women are most fertile the thick mucus becomes watery
- Methods of fertilization
  - Aside from the traditional form of fertilization (intercourse) there are a few options for those struggling with infertility:
    - **Artificial insemination**
      - Sperm is put into the woman's reproductive tract by any means aside from sexual intercourse.
    - **In vitro fertilization**

- - - Sperm and egg are fertilized outside the womb and are re-inserted into the womb in hopes of implantation.
    - When the egg and sperm are combined during this process it is called **intracytoplasmic sperm injection** (when a single sperm is inserted into a single egg).
  - **Gamete intrafallopian transfer (GIFT)**
    - Egg is removed from the ovary and inserted into the fallopian tube. Sperm is also put in the fallopian tube in hopes the fertilization will take place inside the woman's body.

PREGNANCY

- The typical signs of pregnancy are:
  - Missed menstruation
  - Nausea
  - Tender and enlarged breasts
  - Darkening of the areola (nipple area)
  - Increased urination
  - Fetal movement
- **Birth**
  - Labor occurs in three stages:
    - **Effacement** and **dilation** of the cervix occurs when the cervix opens (dilation) and thins (effacement).
      - Early labor is considered a dilation of less than three centimeters.

- A thick mucus discharge (called a **bloody show**) may be apparent as well as contractions.
- During active labor, the cervix has dilated to almost seven centimeters with close contractions (less than five minutes apart).
- Active labor lasts usually between three and eight hours.
- **Transition** occurs in the first stage when the cervix dilates from seven to ten centimeters. This is the shortest, but most strenuous part of labor. The average transition phase lasts between fifteen minutes and three hours.
  - The second stage is the **birth**. Once the baby's head is delivered its airway is cleared and the body follows shortly thereafter.
  - The final stage, delivery of the placenta, happens about five to ten minutes after the baby is born. Mild contractions occur as the uterus expels the placenta.

DEVELOPMENT BY TRIMESTER

- **First trimester**
  - The sperm and egg combine and each carry 23 chromosomes.
  - As the chromosomes fuse into 46 the genetic traits (hair, eye color, sex) are determined.
  - In the fourth week the circulatory system begins to develop, and by the fifth week the fetus has a beating heart.
  - The circulatory system is the first system to develop.

- o In week nine, the fetus begins to develop the reproductive organs.
- o In the final week of the first trimester the fingers and toes are already apparent and begin to grow nails.

- **Second trimester**
    - o Begins at week 13
    - o After week 12 the likelihood of a miscarriage decreases exponentially.
    - o Skin begins to form, the fetus can hear, and taste buds develop.
    - o By the end of the second trimester the fetus' lungs, liver, and immune system are not completely developed; however, there is an 85 percent survival rate for babies born in the 27th week.

- **Third trimester**
    - o Final trimester, and the lungs, liver and immune system finish developing.
    - o The fetus begins to get larger.
    - o The lungs are the last organ to properly develop; therefore babies born prematurely often need steroids and assistance breathing in the Neonatal Intensive Care Unit (NICU).

Pregnancy accompanies a great many tests during prenatal care. One of the many is an amniocentesis. An **amniocentesis** is when a needle is injected into the abdomen, and amniotic fluid is withdrawn for testing. The amniotic fluid is tested for genetic, neural, and chromosomal issues. Some of the medical complications tested for during the amniocentesis are:

- **Cystic fibrosis** (fatal mucus disease)
- **Spina bifida** (spine doesn't close properly)
- **Down syndrome** (Trisomy 21)
    - The 21st chromosome has three instead of two.
    - It is characterized by a flat facial profile, heart problems, delayed development, small ears, large tongue, and upward slanted eyes.
- **Tay-Sachs** (fatal lipid disorder)
    - Fatal disorder where the nerve cells are distended with fatty material and mental and physical disabilities result.
    - People with Tay-Sachs also have cherry-red spots in their eyes.
    - Both man and woman must carry the mutated gene for a child to inherit it.

The amniocentesis can pinpoint with significant accuracy the presence of a condition, but cannot tell the severity of it. The tests are done for several reasons; personal, medical intervention that can improve the life of a child later (the effects of spina bifida can be minimized with a prenatal surgery), decision to carry the fetus to term, or the preparation of living with a special needs child.

The mother is also tested for a variety of conditions:

- **Gestational diabetes**
    - Temporary diabetic condition that can usually be managed by healthy food choices to control glucose levels.

- **Anemia**
    - Iron deficiency that can slow baby growth or trigger labor.

- **Group B strep**
    - Bacteria that may be found in the vagina or rectum.
    - Not harmful to adults, but can cause a major infection to the baby.
    - If there is a positive test for Group B strep an antibiotic is administered during labor.

SEXUALITY

Sexual response follows a specific pattern:

- Excitement
- Plateau
- Orgasmic
- Resolution

There are several different sexual behaviors, including:

- Celibacy (someone who abstains from sex by choice)
- Fantasies and erotic dreams
- Shared touching
- Genital contact (foreplay)
- Oral-genital stimulation (oral sex)
- Intercourse

Some common definitions relating to sexuality are:

- **Psychosocial sexuality**
    - Masculine or feminine traits a person adopts.
- **Gender identification**
    - Ability to recognize and accept self as a male or a female.
- **Androgyny**
    - Blending of gender qualities

SEXUAL ORIENTATION

Sexual orientation refers to what gender the person is, and what gender they are attracted to. There are three sexual orientations:

- Heterosexuals
    - Attracted to the opposite sex.
- Homosexuals
    - Attracted to the same sex.
- Bisexuals
    - Attracted to both sexes.

ALTERNATIVE SEXUAL BEHAVIORS

Other terms that are important to know about sexual behaviors that may be on the test are below:

- **Transsexual**
    - A person rejects his or her own biological identity.
    - Some transsexuals seek sex reassignment operations (an operation to make their biological identity match their emotional one).
- **Transvestite**
    - A person that derives sexual pleasure from dressing like someone from the opposite sex.
- **Fetishism**
    - A person that derives sexual pleasure from either an inanimate object, or a specific part of the body that is typically not sexual.

- **Exhibitionism**
    - A person that derives sexual pleasure from showing off their genitals.
- **Voyeurism** (or "peeping Tom")
    - A person that derives sexual pleasure from watching others that do not know they are being watched.
- **Sadism**
    - A person that derives sexual pleasure from inflicting pain on someone else.
- **Masochism**
    - A person that derives sexual pleasure from receiving pain.
- **Sadomasochism**
    - A person that derives sexual pleasure from both giving and receiving pain.

SEXUALLY DEVIANT BEHAVIORS
- **Zoophylia**
    - Someone who has sex with animals, also known as **bestiality**.
- **Pedophilia**
    - Criminal sexual relations with children. This can also be tied to (but not always), with incest. **Incest** is sex within the family.
- **Rape**
    - Criminal forced sex.
    - Rape is a nondiscriminatory crime; it can happen to women, men, old, or young.

Intimate relationships

People choose to have different levels of intimate relationships. Some people have just one or two deep relationships, while others have several intimate friends. No matter how many, what is important is that the person is capable and shares intimate thoughts, feelings, and emotions.

Communication

Communication can be through verbal and nonverbal means. Most communication is actually nonverbal. We can read a lot from someone's facial expression and stance. There are several ways to improve communication skills:

- **Verbal skills**
    - Think before speaking
    - Focus on the most important pieces
    - Be clear and concise
    - Talk with (not at) the listener
    - Always start positive
    - Seek feedback from the listener to ensure mutual understanding.

- **Listening skills**
    - Focus
    - Select important ideas
    - Provide feedback to the person to ensure mutual understanding.
    - Listen twice as much as you speak.

- Nonverbal communication skills
    - Comfortably touch people

- Keep an appropriate distance
- Assume a non-threatening stance
- Dress appropriately
- Maintain eye contact
- Keep an open facial expression

STAGES OF ATTRACTION AND KINDS OF LOVE

There are several stages of attraction, including:

- **Marketing**
  - Initial stage of relationship
  - When finding new friends, acquaintances and co-workers we also market to be the best version of ourselves.

- **Sharing**
  - Belief systems, commonalities, and values are shared.
  - If there is enough compatibility during the sharing stage, then the typical relationship moves to the behavior stage.

- **Behavior**
  - During the behavior stage one of two things develop passionate love or friendship.
    - **Passionate love**
      - Characterized as a transitory phase of intense feelings and attraction.
      - Passionate love doesn't last very long, it is also known as infatuation or lust.
      - Passionate love usually gives way to companionate love.

- **Companionate love**
  - Less intense, characterized as a deep, enduring attachment built on mutual empathy, support, and tolerance.
  - Friendship and marriage are characterized by many of the same feelings of companionate love (trust, tolerance, and empathy).
- Helen Fisher has a second theory of love in her book, <u>Why We Love: The Nature and Chemistry of Romantic Love,</u> she theorizes that the human brain has three systems for love:
  - **Lust**
    - Sex drive or libido
  - **Attraction**
    - Early, intense romance of love
  - **Attachment**
    - Deep feelings of union with someone long term

Healthy Aging

Healthy aging consists of growing into a productive adult, coping with midlife and facing mortality in a positive and healthy way.

Becoming an Adult

Growing adults try to reinforce their inner identity by acting the same on the outside. A significant interest in "striking out on one's own" develops during the maturation process. Growing adults satisfy their need for independence through:

- Friendships
- Marriage
- Travel
- Military
- College

Midlife

Not everyone has a midlife crisis. In fact many do not. However, there is a general feeling of starting anew in midlife. Midlifers emotionally come to terms with their mortality.

Physically midlifers experience a slow decline in their bodies (bone mass, vertebral compression, loss of lean body mass, vision loss, hearing loss, fertility loss, and a decrease in sexual function). Women experience a sharp decline in their reproduction system through **menopause**. Additionally, women often experience **osteoporosis** (the loss of calcium from bone). Both genders experience **osteoarthritis**, which is a form of arthritis developed from the wear and tear of joint tissue.

Elderly

During the final years of life a greater concentration is put on maintaining physical function and independence wherever possible:

- **Rehabilitation**
    - Returning function to a previous level (i.e. teaching someone that recently broke their hip to walk again).
- **Remediation**
    - Restoring function through alternative methods (i.e. providing a wheelchair to restore mobility without restoring walking).

Some elderly people experience Alzheimer's disease. **Alzheimer's disease** is an organic brain syndrome in which the sufferer experiences memory loss, confusion, loss of reasoning, brain degeneration, dementia, and ultimately death.

Death and bereavement

There are some common sense rules when dealing with dying people, but unfortunately we find death so uncomfortable that they bear mentioning. When dealing with dying people, be genuine, cry if you need to, don't fill silences with empty talk, and be there for the person.

Euthanasia

There are two types of euthanasia.

- **Direct euthanasia**
    - Typically accomplished through an overdose of prescription drugs for pain.

- **Passive euthanasia**
    - Typically by removing life saving devices (feeding tube, bypass machine).

Dr. Jack Kevorkian has championed euthanasia and a terminal patient's right to die. He has assisted many people in death, and ultimately paid the price by going to prison for eight years.

Hospice care

Hospice care is a facility that doesn't focus on "curing" someone that is terminally ill. The facility focuses on comfort, and the right to die with dignity. These facilities offer respite for the family members that have been caring for a dying person.

Bereavement

Kubler-Ross outlined the process of grieving. There are five stages of grieving:

- **Denial**
    - Refusal to accept the facts or information on a situation.

- **Anger**
  - Manifests differently depending on the person. They may be angry with themselves or others close to them.

- **Bargaining**
  - Attempt to bargain or compromise.

- **Depression** (aka preparatory grieving)
  - An acceptance with emotional attachment.

- **Acceptance**
  - Some emotional detachment sets in and sometimes when someone is dying they reach this stage before those around them do.

WHAT YOU CAN DO TO PREPARE FOR THE INEVITABLE

Some things to think about to make it easier for your family to make important decisions are:

- **Anatomical donations**
  - Donation of body parts usually indicated on a driver's license.

- **Orders**
  - Do Not Resuscitate
  - Comfort Measures Only

- **Wills** and other legal documents

PART III. SUBSTANCE USE AND ABUSE

Substance use and abuse will account for approximately ten percent of the exam. This section will focus on the most common topics, however once you have studied this, you may want to purchase the Substance Abuse study guide for the next DANTES test (ACE recommends three upper level credits).

When substances are used a physical and/or psychological dependence and tolerance develop.

- **Physical dependence**
    - Most dangerous
    - Body relies on the substance to perform normal functions.
    - Abstinence of the drug can produce significant withdrawal symptoms such as:
        - Irritability
        - Depression
        - Pain
        - Death
- **Psychological dependence** (or habituation)
    - Intense desire to continue using the drug.
- **Tolerance**
    - Increased doses are necessary to get the same "high".
    - **Cross tolerance**
        - Development of tolerance from drugs that are in the same family.

There is a fundamental difference between substance misuse and substance abuse.

- **Substance misuse**
    - Inappropriate use of drugs for medication.
- **Substance abuse**
    - Use of any drug that has an adverse affect on health.

ALCOHOL

Alcohol is created from the fermentation process of grains or fruit.

- The product of yeast and the sugars is a substance called **ethanol** or **ethyl alcohol**.

- **Proof** Is the measurement of how much alcohol is in a drink.
    - Proof is expressed as half of the total amount of a beverage.
    - Proof is typically a measurement for the liquors.

Alcohol is also commonly known as "liquid courage" or "social lubricant" because its intoxicating ingredients make people more outgoing, relaxed, adventuresome, and forgetful of their inhibitions. Many believe that alcohol is a stimulant; however, alcohol is a depressant.

EFFECTS OF ALCOHOL

The factors that relate to the rate of alcohol absorption are:

- Strength of alcohol
- Number of drinks
- How closely drinks are consumed
- Emptiness of the stomach
- Size of person

The blood alcohol concentration (BAC) rises when the liver cannot oxidize it. The graph on the next page shows examples of typical behavior related to BAC levels.

BAC level	Behaviors
.05% (1/2 part alcohol to every 1000 part blood)	Inhibitions are less stringent, and the everyday worries of life are released ("buzzed")
.1% (1 part alcohol to every 1000 part blood)	May not feel intoxicated, but the individual loses some coordination (most states consider this legally intoxicated)
.2% (2 part alcohol to every 1000 part blood)	This is the obnoxious drunk at the party, may be boisterous, loud, aggressive, and staggering
BAC level	**Behaviors**
.3% (3 part alcohol to every 1000 part blood)	Comprehension is compromised severely and will likely be unable to communicate coherent thoughts.
.4-.5% (4-5 part alcohol to every 1000 part blood)	DANGER! Risk of fatal intoxication (alcohol poisoning). Central Nervous System begins to shut down and brain activity slows.

Symptoms of Alcohol Poisoning

Alcohol poisoning (acute alcohol intoxication) is a potentially fatal condition that is caused by the rapid increase in the BAC level due to consumption of alcoholic beverages. The symptoms of alcohol poisoning are:

- Unconsciousness
- Weak and rapid pulse (>100 beats per minute)
- Clammy skin
- Bluish hue to the skin
    - For darker pigments the nail beds will be an indication of the blue tint.

Any person suffering from alcohol poisoning will need immediate medical attention. They need to be carefully observed while waiting for medical help to arrive. A complication of alcohol poisoning is **asphyxiation** (lack of oxygen to the brain) by choking on vomit.

Alcohol Related Health Issues

Alcohol has significant health consequences in pregnancy. When alcohol crosses into the fetus (through the placenta) the fetus' liver is unable to properly oxidize the alcohol resulting in toxic effects. Fetal alcohol syndrome can occur in babies that have been exposed to alcohol. The characteristics of **fetal alcohol syndrome** are

- Low birth weight
- Mental retardation
- Learning disabilities
- Joint problems
- Heart problems
- Small head

- Widely set eyes

Fetal alcohol syndrome is irreversible and totally avoidable by abstaining from alcohol during pregnancy.

Cirrhosis is another complication for the long time drinker. The alcohol will eventually impair circulation of the liver as the liver and kidneys begin to breakdown. This condition can be fatal (without a transplant).

Alcohol related social issues

There are also social issues directly related to alcohol abuse. A direct correlation between accidents, crime and violence, suicide and alcohol can be drawn.

There are several organizations that are related to curbing alcohol abuse:

- **Alcoholics Anonymous** (AA)
- **Mothers Against Drunk Driving (MADD)**
    - Funded by Candy Lightner after her daughter was killed in 1980.
- **Students Against Drunk Driving (SADD)**
    - A group that focuses on high school students that enforces a contractual agreement between parent and child.

Problem drinking is when someone doesn't need drinks to support body functions (they aren't psychologically or physically addicted), but when they do drink they cause problems for themselves or others.

Alcoholism

Alcoholism is a complex disease; it has both psychological and physical symptoms. Alcoholics must drink for their body to operate normally. Alcohol withdrawals include:

- Shaking
- Nausea

- Vomiting
- Occasionally hallucinations
- Shock
- Cardiac and pulmonary arres
- **Delirium tremens** (DT)
    - An occasional withdrawal symptom of hallucinations paired with shaking.

There are psychological factors of alcoholism:

- **Denial**
    - When the alcoholic cannot admit that they have a problem and that life is normal.
- **Enabling**
    - Loved ones inability to admit the alcoholic has a problem.
- Children and spouses of alcoholics are typically labeled as **co-dependents** of alcohol.

Adult Children of Alcoholics (ACOA) exhibit similar traits across personality types. While not always the case, ACOA's typically have problems with:

- Having fun
- Change
- Follow through
- Self-forgiveness

TOBACCO

While it may soon be overcome by obesity, by the publishing date of this book smoking was the number one cause of premature deaths in the United States. All forms of tobacco are unhealthy and develop physical and emotional dependence. Tobacco forms include:

- Pipes
- Cigars
- Chew
- Cigarettes

Those that smoke pipes, cigars, and chew have a greater chance of cancer of the mouth and throat areas. Smoking increases lung cancer, cardiovascular disease (myocardial infarction- heart attack), and respiratory ailments. While most people become dependent on smoking, there are a few, called "**chippers**" that can smoke a couple of cigarettes a day without dependence.

People smoke for different reasons such as:

- Peer pressure
- Ability to control a situation
- Self-medication
- Influenced by advertising

Nicotine (the addictive ingredient in tobacco) stimulates neurotransmitters to create arousal feelings. However, in larger doses the central nervous system begins to slow, creating feelings of relaxation.

One of the effects of oral tobacco is the development of white leathery patches on your gums, tongue, and inside cheeks in a condition called **Leukoplakia.** This condition can be a serious sign of cancer (or totally benign).

The Compounds of the Cigarette

The two phases of cigarettes are particulate and gaseous.

- **Particulate**
    - Composed of the particles of the cigarette; nicotine, water, and the chemical compounds (tar).

- **Gaseous**
    - The smoke (carbon monoxide)

The small hairs (called **cilia**) that line the nose and ears become clogged with cigarette particulates making them less effective. The body produces a hacking cough to try to effectively get the mucus out.

Smoking and the Blood

The carbon monoxide that smoking generates combines with red blood cells in a process called **carboxyhemoglobin** that renders the blood cell unable to move oxygen through the system. This condition is irreversible for red blood cells, and they are useless for the entirety of their lifecycle (120 days). This condition also causes clotting problems.

Other Complications of Tobacco Use

- **COLD (Chronic Obstructive lung Disease)**
    - Inflammation or infection of the small airways that go into the lungs.

- **Pulmonary emphysema**
    - Non-curable disease that destroys the **aleveoli** (sacs where the air is transferred into the blood).
    - Those that suffer pulmonary emphysema are almost always elderly people that have spent many years smoking.

Smoking also affects reproduction in a variety of ways. Smoking can cause low sperm motility and lower hormone levels for women. Additionally, when smoking while pregnant the carboxyhemoglobin literally suffocates the fetus. Carboxyhemoglobin increases the likelihood of stillborns, miscarriages, lower birth rate, and sudden infant death syndrome (SIDS). Finally, smoking mixed with oral contraception can be deadly. The birth control pill and smoking increases the risk of stroke and heart attack.

OTHER DRUGS

The following drugs are identified with their "street names" and their effects.

- **Cocaine** (coke)
    - The strongest stimulant and is derived from the coca plant native to South America.
    - When snorted it is called **coke.**
    - When smoked it is either **freebase** (use of powder cocaine chemically altered and smoked through a pipe) or **crack** (coke mixed with baking soda that dries into rocklike crystals inhaled through a pipe).
    - Cocaine is an expensive habit because the effects of the drug last only from 5-30 minutes.
    - During the "high" there is a feeling of exhilaration.
- **Crystal meth** (ice)
    - The most dangerous methamphetamine.
    - Within seven seconds of ingestion the effect is felt, and it lasts for several hours (basically until the user can no longer physically sustain the high).
    - Chronic use of crystal meth causes:
        - Weight loss
        - Compromised immunity system
        - Damages major organs
- **Barbiturates**
    - Drugs used to depress the central nervous system to calm down or sleep.
    - Medically they are used for:

- - - Anesthesia
    - Anxiety disorders
    - Insomnia
    - Epilepsy
  - Some common barbiturates names are:
    - Methaqualone
    - Quaalude ("ludes")
    - Sopor
- **Tranquilizers**
  - Reduces anxiety, relaxes people that are having trouble coping with their lives or may have suffered a great shock that they are incapable of handling (i.e. sudden unexpected death of a loved one).
  - The major difference between barbiturates and tranquilizers are that tranquilizers are used to help cope during waking hours, while barbiturates are primarily designed to cause sleep.
  - Some common tranquilizer names are:
    - Valium (diazepam)
    - Librium (chloridiazepoxide)
- **Hallucinogens**
  - Produce perceived distortions in reality.
  - The most common types are:
    - Lysergic acid diethylamide (LSD) (acid)
    - Mescaline (from peyote cactus plant)

- Psilocybin (mushroom, or shrooms)
- Can cause synesthesia, which is the mixing of senses (i.e. being able to hear a painting, or taste a song).
- Do not cause a physical addiction; however there have been reports of mild psychological addictions.
- A very dangerous hallucinogen is **phencyclidine** (PCP, "angel dust") which has unpredictable affects that can cause euphoria, bizarre perceptions, paranoia, aggression, and can be stored in the cells for many months after ingestion.

- **Cannabis** (marijuana)
    - Plant, where the dried leaves can be put in pipes, or rolled up in cigarette paper (joints).
    - Additionally, the resin from the tops of the flowers yields **hash** that can be smoked in a pipe, which has a much stronger effect than the leaf itself.

- **Narcotics**
    - Strong drugs that cause the most dependence.
    - There are three types:
        - Natural
            - Typically used from pain treatment (**analgesics**).
            - Produced from the Oriental poppy and include:
                - Opium
                - Morphine
                - Thebaine

- Quasi-synthetic
  - The opiates are chemically altered (e.g. morphine is chemically altered into heroin).
- Synthetic.
  - Same family as the natural ones, but are made completely in a lab.
  - They include:
    - Meperiden (Demerol, propoxyphene)
      - Usually prescribed for post surgery pain.
    - Darvon
      - Usually prescribed for post surgery pain.
    - Methadone
      - Methadone is used to help heroin addicts wean off of the drug.

- **Inhalants**
  - Produce drunk-life effects very quickly and cheaply.
  - Common household items can be inhaled (gasoline, paint, paint thinner).
  - Highly volatile and can cause death.

TYPES OF DRUGS

Drugs are categorized by the effects they have on the system. Some drugs fit into more than one category because of their effects.

- **Psychoactive drugs** (psychotropic drugs) can be:
    - Stimulants
    - Depressants
    - Hallucinogens
    - Opiates
    - Inhalants
    - Identified by their ability to change behavior, feelings, perceptions, and moods.

- **Stimulants**
    - Excite the nervous system.
    - AKA "uppers"
    - Physical effects such as:
        - Increased heart beat
        - Increased blood pressure
        - Heightened brain function
    - Some examples of stimulants are:
        - Cocaine
        - Caffeine
        - Amphetamines
            - Completely manufactured
            - Increase activity and elevate mood

- Medically a treatment for **narcolepsy** (sleeping disorder) and obesity.
    - Methamphetamines
        - Drugs similar chemically to amphetamines, but stronger.
        - Street names include:
            - Crank
            - Ice
            - Crystal
            - Meth
            - Speed
            - Zip
    - Dependence and tolerance of stimulants happens quickly.
- **Depressants**
    - Slow the central nervous system
    - AKA "downers"
    - Drugs in this category include:
        - Alcohol
        - Barbiturates
        - Tranquilizers
- **Designer drugs**
    - AKA "club drugs"
    - Produce mild hallucinogenic effects.
    - Some examples are:

- Synthetic heroin (MPPP)
- Ecstasy (MDMA)

THE EFFECTS OF COMBINING DRUGS

There are three possible effects from combining drug use.

- **Additive**
    - Drugs combine in the system, but do not exaggerate one another.

- **Antagonistic**
    - One drug cancels the effect of another.

- **Potentiated**
    - One drug actually intensifies the effect of another.
    - The potentiated effects of drugs have caused many unplanned emergencies and deaths.

HERBAL REMEDIES

Below are some common herbal supplements and their effects.

- **Echinacea**
    - Native Americans used Echinacea as a general cure all.
    - It has been used to treat scarlet fever, syphilis, malaria, and blood poisoning.
    - Today's use of Echinacea is for reducing the symptoms of flu and cold, and as an immune booster.

- **Ginkgo biloba**
    - Typically its use is in the extracted state.
    - It is used to treat circulatory disorders and enhance memory.
    - Scientific studies suggest Ginkgo may be effective in increasing blood flow to the brain of elderly individual.
    - Ginkgo can also improve blood circulation by dilating the vessels and reducing the adhesive components of the blood platelets.
    - Ginkgo has **flavanoids** and **terpenoids** that are considered antioxidants.
        - **Antioxidants** neutralize free radicals.
            - **Free radicals** are compounds that alter cell membranes, damage DNA, and can cause death.
            - Free radicals are natural in the body, but can be increased by environmental factors (pollution, smoking, ultraviolet light, and radiation).

- Free radicals are contributors to heart disease, Alzheimer's disease, and dementia.

- **Milk Thistle** (silybum marianum)
    - Used for liver problems, protect the liver from viruses, toxins, alcohol and acetaminophen (aspirin).
    - Some testing has also indicated that milk thistle can inhibit the growth of cancer.

- **St. John's Wort** (hypericum perforatum)
    - Used in ancient Greece to treat a range of nervous conditions.
    - It also has antibacterial, antiviral, and anti-inflammatory properties that can help heal wounds and burns.
    - Scientific research suggests St. John's Wort can help with depression symptoms as well.

PART IV. FITNESS AND NUTRITION

The fitness and nutrition component of this test will make up 15 percent of the questions. There are five components to physical fitness:

- Cardio respiratory endurance
- Muscular strength
- Muscular endurance
- Flexibility
- Body composition

While there is much controversy on how often you should work out, the general rule is 3-5 times a week, between 20 and 60 minutes long. Resistance (strength) training should be done at least twice a week.

A true indicator of aerobic activity is to calculate the **target heart rate**. The formula for target heart rate is:

- 220 which is the maximum heart rate (MHR) subtracted by age.
- 60-90% of that number is the target heart rate:
    - Example: A 20 year old should use the following formula:

        220 (MHR) – 20 (age) = 200 (MHR adjusted for age)

        200 * .6 = 120 (60% of MHR) to 200 * .9 = 180 (90% of MHR)

    - A heart rate between 120 and 180 beats per minute for a 20 year old is considered their target heart rate for exercise.

To take the pulse the pointer and middle finger should be placed at the carotid artery (beside the Adam's apple). Be careful to not measure with a thumb because the thumb will also generate a pulse.

Two types of exercise

The two types of exercise are:

- **Aerobic**
    - Body can supply the oxygen needed to all body parts.
- **Anaerobic**
    - The body cannot be oxygenated fast enough to supply the energy needed from oxygen alone.
    - Typically anaerobic energy is not reached until the body is at high intensity.
    - The maximum amount of oxygen that will chemically combine with hemoglobin is the **oxygen capacity**.

Muscles

Strength training improves physical fitness. By increasing muscle mass, the body will need more energy to sustain life. There are three ways to improve muscle strength:

- **Isometric**
    - Static exercises that focus solely on resistance (e.g. pushing against a wall).
    - Since isometric exercises are difficult to measure, they are not used much in strength training routines.
- **Progressive resistance**
    - Progressive resistance (*isotonic*) exercises are the use of traditional free weights that provide a fixed resistance.
- **Isokinetic**
    - Exercises use a range of motion through mechanical device to provide resistance.

OBESITY

There is little argument that people's waistlines (in developed countries) are quickly expanding. There are several theories for the expansion of today's waistlines:

- **Genetics**
    - Inheriting of tendencies to become big; sometimes it is the sole reason (thyroid issues and other endocrine system issues).
    - In other instances, genetics is simply a contributing factor (slow metabolism).
- The **set-point theory**
    - The body "likes" a current weight, which makes it very difficult for the person to go beneath that weight.
- Babies that are overfed may develop more fat cells (**hypercellular obesity**) making them more susceptible to weight gain as adults.
- As an adult if you typically eat more than you expend, then the fat cells will begin to grow to accommodate the increased intake (**hypertrophic obesity**).
- Growing older also can contribute to obesity. The body needs less energy to sustain life.

SLIMMING DOWN

People try to remedy obesity in one of three ways:

- Diet modification
    - Almost always a part of a successful weight loss program.
    - Eating a balanced diet with realistic portions is the most realistic and healthy way to control weight.
    - Fad diets (rarely successful), low-calorie diet, controlled fasting (not recommended), and self-help (Jenny Craig,

Weight Watchers, etc) are other methods of diet modification.

- Physical intervention
    - Introducing something into the body to help control food intake (e.g. appetite suppressants).
- Behavior intervention
    - Includes hypnosis and increased physical activity.

The most successful way to lose weight is a common sense combination approach, eating better and less, accompanied with increasing physical activity.

Eating disorders are not a way to lose weight; they will damage your body. The two types of eating disorders are:

- Bulimia nervosa
    - **Bulimics** will gorge and purge (in the process destroying their esophagus over time).
- Anorexia nervosa
    - **Anorexics** will avoid eating altogether (sometimes until the point of death).

Good nutrition and its effects

Sources of nutrients

Food is divided into five categories:

- **Carbohydrates**
    - Used for energy
    - Can be either sugars or starches

- **Fats**
    - Used for energy
    - Denser than carbohydrates

- **Proteins**
    - In every living cell of the body
    - A high quality protein has all nine essential amino acids (building blocks of cells)
    - High quality protein is typically found in animal products.
    - Incomplete proteins can be combined with others to form a complete protein.

- **Vitamins**
    - No calories
    - Needed for normal growth and reproduction
    - Two kinds of vitamins
        - Water soluble
            - Water-soluble includes the B and C vitamins.
            - Overdose of water-soluble vitamins are extracted through urine.
        - Fat-soluble

- Fat-soluble vitamins include vitamins A, D, E, and K.
- These vitamins are stored in liver and fat where the excess accumulates until it can be taken out.

- **Minerals**
    - Not organic and are used for a variety of very important functions including:
        - Teeth
        - Muscles
        - Hormones
        - Heart function
        - Red cell formation
    - There are 21 minerals used for human development, the most important are:
        - Calcium
        - Phosphorus
        - Sulfur
        - Sodium
        - Potassium
        - Magnesium
    - Five percent of the body is made of up minerals.

The importance of water and fiber cannot be overstated.

- Without water we would die in less than a week.
- More than half of the human body is made up of water.

- An adult needs between 6-10 glasses a day.
- **Fiber**
    - Indigestible plant material
    - There are two types:
        - Soluble
            - The soluble fiber turns into a kind of gel in the tract and binds to cholesterol moving it out of the system.
        - Insoluble
            - Can absorb water while in the digestive tract.
            - It adds bulk to stools and helps digestion.

THE FOOD GROUPS

The food groups received a makeover recently from the Federal Drug Administration (FDA). The FDA has determined that not everyone is built the same and needs the same amount of food. Additional information on the new food pyramid can be found at the FDA sponsored website at www.mypyramid.gov.

FIGURE 2

The general rules are:

- Make smart choices from all food groups.
- Find balance between diet and exercise.
- Choose nutritionally dense foods.
- Stay within caloric needs.

In the new food pyramid from left to right are the following food groups:

- Grains
    - Includes foods that are made from wheat, rice, oats, cornmeal, barley, or other cereal grain products.
    - Common examples of the "grain group" are bread, pasta, cereals, and tortillas.
    - Grains have two subgroups; whole grains and refined grains.
        - **Whole grains** are the entire grain kernel (bran, germ, endosperm).
            - Examples of whole grain products are; whole wheat flour, bulgur, oatmeal, and brown rice.
        - **Refined grains** are milled and the process removes the bran and germ.
            - Grains are milled to change the texture and extend their shelf life; however, it comes at a cost the milling process removing the dietary fiber, iron, and many B vitamins.
                - Examples of refined grains are; white flour, degermed cornmeal, white bread, and white rice.
                - Refined grains are typically enriched. **Enriched** means that some of the B

vitamins (thiamin, riboflavin, niacin, folic acid) and iron are added back in.
- Fiber is not added back in during the enrichment process.
- Vegetables
  - There are five subgroups based on their nutrients.
    - Dark green (broccoli, collard greens)
    - Orange (pumpkin, sweet potatoes, carrots)
    - Starchy (corn, peas, lima beans)
    - Dry beans and peas (black beans, kidney beans, black-eyed peas)
    - Other vegetables (asparagus, artichokes)
- Fruits
  - Fruits have a group of their own in the new pyramid.
  - Fruit groups include:
    - Citrus
    - Berries
    - Others
- Oils
  - The oil group is the fats that are liquid at room temperature.
  - Some examples of foods in the oil group are:
    - Canola oil
    - Mayonnaise
    - Some salad dressing

- - Margarine
  - No food (including fats) from plant sources contains cholesterol.
  - Solid fats are fats that are solid at room temperature (butter, shortening).
- Milk
  - The milk group includes all products that are made from milk that retain their calcium.
  - Products that are made from milk but have very little calcium (cream cheese and butter) are not considered a part of this group.
  - Most choices in the milk group should be lower fat.
  - Some examples of milk choices are; milk, pudding, cheese, yogurt, and ice cream.
- Meat and beans
  - The meat and beans group includes:
    - All foods from animal sources
    - Dry beans
    - Eggs
    - Nuts
    - Seeds
  - The dry beans and peas are in this group and the vegetable group.
  - Making lean choices is important to maintain a healthy lifestyle.

There are 2800 kinds of food additives that the FDA has approved for use. Food additives improve the texture, shelf life, consistency, and taste of foods.

VEGETARIANS

There are three types of vegetarians:

- Ovolactovegetarian
    - Eat eggs and dairy/milk but no other animal products.
- Lactovegetarian
    - Eat dairy/milk but no other animal products.
- Vegan
    - Eat no animal or animal by-products.

Vegetarians (especially vegans) need to closely watch their diets to ensure they do not have vitamin or protein deficiencies.

Part V. Risk Factors, Disease, and Disease Prevention

Risk factors, disease, and disease prevention account for twenty percent of the exam questions.

Infectious Diseases, Including Sexually Transmitted Diseases, Prevention and Control

Necessary Components of a Disease

In order to contract an infectious disease the following are needed:

- **Agent**
  - Diseases begin as a **pathogen**, which is a disease-producing agent.
  - The pathogen can be bacterial, fungal, or viral.

- **Entry point**
  - Two modes of transmission (entry point) of the pathogen are direct and indirect.
    - **Direct transmission** is passed via bodily fluids, droplets, and feces.
    - **Indirect transmission** is passed via inanimate objects and nonhuman living things (fleas, ticks, mosquitoes).

- **Reservoir**
  - For a disease to be successfully contracted the host needs to be able to give the pathogen a place to live (i.e. bloodstream) or a reservoir.

- **Exit point**
  - The disease must have an exit portal to leave the system and infect others.

- o A cough or sneeze would be a successful exit point for a cold pathogen.

A note about viruses: Viruses are not alive. A virus must exist within a living cell so it can replicate. A virus has genes made form DNA or RNA, which is what enables the replication inside the living cell. However, the virus cannot exist outside the cell.

INFECTIOUS STAGES

There are four basic stages to an infection.

- **Incubation** (silent stage)
    - o Symptoms are typically not present.
    - o While it is possible to infect others in this stage it is not likely.
- **Prodromal**
    - o The pathogen multiplies rapidly in this stage.
    - o During the prodromal stage the host will likely experience some symptoms and are more likely to infect others.
- **Peak** (acme)
    - o Symptoms are the most intense and it is the most contagious phase of the disease.
- **Recovery** (convalescent)
    - o The body begins to heal from the disease.

IMMUNE SYSTEM RESPONSE

The body has two lines of defense against infection.

- **Mechanical**
    - Skin mucus, earwax, and tears
- **Cellular**
    - Immune system
    - The major components of the immune system are:
        - When the **antigens** (infection) are introduced the first line are the **microphages** (large white blood cells).
        - The microphages will kill some of the antigens, but if that doesn't work the microphages call in for help to the **helper t-cells**.
        - The helper t-cells are the "messengers" of the group; they call to arms the **killer t-cells** and the **b-cells**.
        - The killer t-cells will activate specific types of white blood cells that are best suited to kill the antigen, and the b-cells transform into cells that produce antibodies that inactivate the antigen by clumping them together.
        - While the war is raging with the killer t-cells and the b-cells, the **memory t-cells** and **suppressor t-cells** form to "remember" the immune system's response to the antigen to discourage re-infection, or in the event of a re-infection to recover quickly.
        - The suppressor t-cells reign in the b-cells so that once the battle is won the antibodies will cease production.

KINDS OF IMMUNITY

There are three kinds of immunity; naturally acquired, artificially acquired, and passively acquired.

- **Naturally acquired immunity** (NAI)
    - Body fights an infection, and develops a "memory" of it to prevent reinfection (Chicken Pox).

- **Artificially acquired immunity** (AAI)
    - Body develops immunity from a vaccination or immunization (flu shot).

- **Passively acquired immunity** (PAI)
    - Antibodies are used until the body can supply a natural form of immunity against an infection.

COMMON INFECTIOUS DISEASES

- Common cold (**acute rhinitis**)
    - Highly contagious respiratory tract infection that is the most infectious human disease. The symptoms of a common cold include:
        - Runny nose
        - Watery eyes
        - General aches
        - Slight fever
    - The best offense against the common cold is frequent hand washing.

- Flu (**influenza**)
    - Common infectious disease

- The flu is caused by a virus (therefore typically the flu has to "run its course").
- Symptoms of the flu are:
  - Chills
  - Fever
  - Cough
  - Aches
  - Pains
  - Sore throat
  - Headache
  - Gastrointestinal issues.
- The best offense against the flu is frequent hand washing.

- **Tuberculosis** (TB)
  - Less common, but more serious infectious disease.
  - TB travels by air and is common in crowded places.
  - Healthy people are typically able to contain the infection and prevent infection to others, but someone who is immune compromised can become infected and transmit the infection.

- **Pneumonia**
  - Variety of respiratory conditions that can be:
    - Bacterial
    - Viral
    - Fungal

- o The elderly or those that are immune compromised (HIV+) can be susceptible to succumbing to a pneumonia infection.
- **Mononucleosis**
  - o An infectious illness that produces a number of mononuclear leukocytes.
  - o The symptoms to mononucleosis are:
    - Weakness
    - Fatigue
    - Swollen lymph glands (especially around the throat)
    - Sore throat
  - o This disease is caused by a strain of the Epstein-Barr virus.
  - o The treatment consists of pain medication, plenty of fluids, and bed rest.
  - o Subsequent infections are unlikely because infection causes a natural acquired immunity.
- **Chronic fatigue syndrome** (CFS)
  - o Most susceptible to women in their 30s and 40s.
  - o The symptoms consist of:
    - Flu like symptoms
    - Severe exhaustion
    - Fatigue
    - Headaches
    - Muscle aches
    - Fever
    - Inability to concentrate

- Allergies
- Intolerance to exercise
- Depression

- **Measles** (rubella)
  - Highly contagious and short lived (about a week).
  - The symptoms consist of high fever and a whole body red rash.

- **Mumps**
  - Viral inflammation of the salivary glands.
  - This virus is in the standard form of vaccinations for children.

- **Lyme disease**
  - Disease is a common bacterial disease that is contracted from infected deer ticks or mice.
  - Symptoms include red bumps with a circle rash at the bite site.
  - Lyme disease has two phases.
    - The first phase is flulike.
    - The more serious second phase can cause damage to the nervous system and heart.
      - Phase II can also cause chronic arthritis (lasting 2 years).
      - The immune system does not build immunities against subsequent infection.

Common sexually transmitted diseases

- **AIDS**
  - Acquired Immune Deficiency Syndrome (AIDS) is arguable the most devastating illness in modern times (it is the most serious sexually transmitted disease).
  - AIDS is caused by the **human immunodeficiency virus** (HIV), which attacks the helper t-cells compromising the immunity system.
  - Because the immune system is compromised, HIV patients are susceptible to viral, bacterial, and fungal infections. HIV is spread through blood, semen, vaginal, and perinatal (mother to baby) means.
  - It is not transmitted through saliva, sweat, or tears.
  - At first the person is asymptomatic (no symptoms) during the incubation (could be as little as 6 months to a decade or more).
  - When the person is asymptomatic they are said to be HIV positive. As the symptoms appear and worsen the person is said to have AIDS.
  - There is no cure but there are drugs that can reduce the rate at which the helper t-cells are destroyed.
  - AIDS is preventable by limiting partners, using condoms, avoiding bodily fluids contact, and avoiding drugs that impair judgment.

- **Chlamydia**
  - Sexually transmitted disease that causes painful urination and pus (often times there are no overt symptoms in women).

- o Left untreated Chlamydia can damage reproductive organs and cause arthritis.
- o Treatment does not prevent re-infection.

- **Human papilloma virus** (HPV)
  - o Asymptomatic condition that can cause precancerous cells to grow on the cervix.
  - o Genital warts are also a symptom of infection.
  - o Warts are treated by medication, burning, or freezing.
  - o A vaccine is available to reduce the likelihood of infection.

- **Gonorrhea**
  - o Often asymptomatic in women.
  - o Symptoms are discharge and painful urination.
  - o Gonorrhea is treated with antibiotics.

- **Herpes simplex**
  - o Over 50 viruses.
  - o Some examples are:
    - Chickenpox
    - Shingles
    - Mononucleosis
  - o **Herpes simplex 1** (HSV-1)
    - Labial herpes causes cold sore and blisters on the mouth.
  - o **Herpes simplex 2** (HSV-2)
    - Different strain that causes blisters and lesions on the genitals to prevent the spread of Herpes.

- Transmission is through sex, kissing, and touching an active infection.

- **Syphilis**
    - Caused by bacteria
    - The untreated cycle is as follows:
        - Infection
            - Sufferer is asymptomatic from 10-90 days.
        - Primary stage
            - One to five week period where a small raised, painless chancre appears and heals in four to eight weeks.
        - Secondary stage
            - Sore throat, and loss of hair (in patches)
        - Latent stage
            - Disease is completely asymptomatic, this can last an extended period (15-25 years).
        - Late stage
            - Can recur causing irreversible damage and possibly death.
    - While treatment with antibiotics can kill the infection at any time during the stages, it will not undo the effects of the disease.

The Major Systems of the Body

The four types of structures in the body are:

- **Cells**
    - The simplest units that can maintain life and reproduce.
    - These are the smallest units (that we know of) in the body.
- **Tissues**
    - Groups of similar cells with various materials (living and non living) between them.
- **Organs**
    - Different tissues that work together to perform a function.
    - For example, the stomach is made up of muscle, connective, epithelial, and nervous tissues.
- **Systems**
    - Various organs that perform complex complimentary functions in the body.
    - The ten major systems are:
        - **Skeletal**
            - The skeletal system accounts for approximately 20 percent of body weight.
            - The skeletal system consists of the bones, ligaments, and tendons.
            - Bones protect internal organs and provide a solid support structure that defies gravity.
            - The formation of blood cells (**hematopoiesis**) occurs primarily in the red marrow found inside bones.

- **Muscular**
  - Comprised of muscle fibers that are attached to the bones or organs that are responsible for movement (through contraction).
  - The **skeletal muscles** are attached to the bones through tendons and ligaments and produce movement, facial expression, and respiration.
  - Posture, heat production, and joint stability are all products of the muscular system.
  - Muscles are able to make concentric and eccentric contractions. **Concentric contraction** is when a muscle shortens and develops tension (i.e. the curling of a weight). **Eccentric contraction** is the tension as the muscle lengthens (i.e. the downward movement of a bicep curl).
- **Nervous**
  - Controls, regulates, and communicates
  - The nervous system's major organs are:
    - Brain
    - Spinal cord
    - Nerves
    - Ganglia
  - Nervous system carries out three general functions
    - Sensory

- o Integrative
- o Motor
- The sensor receptors detect internal and external stimuli.
  - o Some examples of external stimuli are temperature, light and sound.
  - o Some examples of internal receptors are pressure, pH, and carbon.
- The sensory information is gathered and converted to electrical signals (**nerve impulses**) that transmit to the brain.
- Decisions are made based on these electrical signals (the decision making process is called **integration**).
- Signals to muscles or glands to respond to the stimuli (motor output function).

- **Endocrine**
  - Regulates **hormones** (molecules that release secretions directly into the blood stream).
  - Hormones influence growth, development, and metabolic activities.
  - The endocrine system contains the glands. There are two categories of glands; exocrine and endocrine.
  - The **exocrine** glands have ducts that carry their product to a surface.
    - o Examples are; sweat, mammary, and digestive enzymes.

- The **endocrine** glands do not have ducts, they secrete directly into the blood where they influence the cells with receptor cites for the specific hormones.

- While the pituitary gland is the "master gland" it is under the control of the hypothalamus.

- The pituitary gland produces a substance called **adrenocorticotropic** (ACTH) that stimulates the adrenal glands to produce corticoids.

- **Corticoids** control glucose, protein, and fat metabolism.

- The **thyroid** gland is in charge of the metabolism (rate of burning energy).

- The **pancreas** has digestive enzymes (insulin) that regulate sugar.

- The **adrenal** glands are made up of two parts (the outer cortex and inner medulla).

- The medulla secretes **epinephrine** (adrenaline) that creates the "flight or fight" response.

- The **gonads** (sex organs) produce the hormones in the reproductive system (estrogen and testosterone).

- The **pineal** gland secretes melatonin that is stimulated by light and induces sleep.

- **Cardiovascular**
  - Also known as the vascular or circulatory system.
  - Transports blood (the adult has about six quarts of blood in the body).
  - The heart, vessels, arteries, veins, and capillaries make up the cardiovascular system.
  - Nutrients and other materials are exchanged throughout the body from the capillaries.
  - Waste products are also removed through the cardiovascular system.
  - The four biggest controllable risk factors for cardiovascular disease are smoking, hypertension, cholesterol levels, and physical activity.
  - The red tubes are the **arteries** (they are red because they are oxygenated).
  - The arteries move away from the heart. The blue tubes are the **veins** that are pumping to the heart (they are going toward the heart to get oxygen).
  - The cardiovascular system matures faster than any other major organ system in fetal development. The developing heart begins to beat regularly about four weeks after fertilization.
  - The cardiovascular system is susceptible to different forms of disease. **Coronary artery**

disease is the damage to the vessels that supply blood to the heart. Coronary heart disease can be caused by **atherosclerosis** (build up of plague on inner walls of heart muscle). A potential warning sign would be when your cholesterol reaches over 200.

- Cholesterol is necessary for human body function; however, too much cholesterol can build up in the arteries. There are two types of cholesterol; low-density lipoproteins (LDL) and high-level lipoproteins (HDL). It is best to keep your LDL (bad cholesterol) under control. The HDL is considered the good cholesterol. Plaque and build up along the inside of the arteries is called **arteriosclerosis**.

- An under oxygenated heart can cause **angina pectoris** (chest pain).

- **Lymphatic**

    - The lymphatic system has three functions: returns excess interstitial fluid into the blood (about 90 percent of fluid that leaves capillary is returned), absorbs fats and fat-soluble vitamins from the digestive system, and defends body against invading pathogens.

    - The lymph nodes and other organs filter the lymph and remove the pathogens.

- **Respiratory**

    - Breath moves from the mouth or nose through the larynx, trachea (a tube) and into the lungs.

- The trachea splits into two tubes (**bronchi**).
- The bronchi divide again into the bronchial tubes that lead into the lungs where they divide again into tiny sacs called **alveoli**.
- The cells that make up the body need oxygen to sustain life.
- The respiratory system works with the circulatory system to supply oxygen, remove waste products, and regulate pH.
- The act of breathing is called **external respiration**, and the blood transporting oxygen to internal tissue cells is **internal respiration**.

- **Digestive**
  - Made up of the organs that break down food until they are small enough to be absorbed for use, or excreted for waste.
  - The gastrointestinal (GI) tract is a long tube from the mouth to the anus. It includes; mouth, pharynx, esophagus, stomach, and the small and large intestine.
  - Digestion and absorption take place in the GI.
  - The digestive system prepares the food for cell use by six functions:
    - **Ingestion** food consumption.
    - **Mechanical ingestion** breaking down large food pieces to smaller ones so enzymes can affect the food particles.

- Begins in the mouth while chewing and continues in the stomach.
  - **Chemical digestion** molecules of foods are broken down into smaller molecules that can be used by cells.
  - **Chemical digestion** happens through **hydrolysis** (a process involving water and digestive enzymes) to break food down.
  - **Movement** is where the food moves into the esophagus (swallowing or **deglutition**).
  - **Absorption** passes through cell membranes in the small intestine to be absorbed in blood or lymph capillaries.
  - **Elimination** removal of unused food through defecation (feces).

- **Urinary**
  - Maintains the volume of fluids within the body and rids the body of waste from cell metabolism.
  - Regulates electrolytes and maintains normal pH levels in the blood.
  - Excretes the hormones **erythropoietin** (controlling red blood cell production) and **rennin** (blood pressure regulator).

- **Reproductive**
  - Four functions:
    - Produce egg and sperm cells
    - Transport and sustain the cells
    - Nurture offspring
    - Produce hormones
  - Three types of organs that make up the reproductive system:
    - **Primary organs** are the gonads; for men this is the testes, and for women the ovaries. They are responsible for producing the egg and sperm cells (**gametes**), and for hormone production.
    - All other pieces of the reproductive system are **secondary** or **accessory** as they are used to transport and sustain gametes, and support the developing offspring.
    - At the time of conception the gender is determined. Sperm determines gender, which is either an X or a Y chromosome. If the sperm is X (X is girl and Y is boy). The woman's ova (egg) are always an X chromosome.
    - For the woman **menstruation** signals the onset of the ability to reproduce and **menopause** signals the end of the reproductive cycle in a woman's life. The time between onset and the end of

the fertile lifecycle in life is much more gradual for men.

o Males reproductive parts consist of; penis, scrotum, testes, seminal vesicles, prostate glands, Cowper's gland. Males are typically not fertile until about age 15. The FSH follicle-stimulating hormone triggers the development of fertile sperm.

o Reproductive system hormones:

- **Estrogen** primarily used in women to; develop breasts, develop uterus and vagina, broaden pelvis, grow pubic hair, and increase fat tissue. It also prepares the body monthly for possible pregnancy, and participates in pregnancy if it occurs. Estrogen synthesis and secretion is stimulated by the **follicle-stimulating hormone** (FSH).

- **Progesterone** is important in pregnancy. Progesterone production is stimulated by the **luteinizing hormone** (LH). LH facilitates the release of the egg from the ovary.

Cancer

Cells die, and when cells are lost, replacement cells are reproduced by the body. This process is monitored by **regulatory genes**. Sometimes these regulatory genes can become cancer genes are **oncogenes** regulatory genes that do not cause cancer are **protooncogenes**. Three reasons why oncogenes develop are:

- Genetic mutations
- Viral infections
- Carcinogens (cancer causing chemicals)

Types of Cancer and Where They Are Found

Cancer is found throughout the body. Treatment options depend on where, what kind, and what stage the cancer is. Some types of cancer are:

- **Carcinoma**
    - Can be on the skin, mouth, throat, intestinal tract, glands, nerves, breasts, urinary, genital structure, lungs, kidneys, or liver.
    - Carcinoma accounts for 85% of all tumors.
- **Sarcoma**
    - Found in the connective tissues (bone, cartilage, tendons).
    - Sarcoma accounts for 2% of cancer cases.
- **Melanoma**
    - Skin cancer caused by sun exposure.
    - ABCD rule recommended by the American Cancer society:
        - **Asymmetric** (not in a circle)
        - **Border irregularity**
        - **Color change**

- - **Diameter** (greater than six millimeters)
- **Neuroblastoma**
  - Starts in immature cells in the central nervous system (typically affects children).
- **Adenocarcinoma**
  - Found in the endocrine glands.
- **Hepatoma**
  - Found in the cells of the liver.
- **Leukemia**
  - Cells in blood (children and adults).
- **Lymphoma**
  - Found in the immune system (lymph nodes) abnormal white cell production and decreased resistance.

Treatment of cancer

There are several types of cancer treatments available. Typically a cancer patient can choose between a few options that range in effectiveness and intrusiveness. The types of treatment are:

- **Surgery**
  - Complete removal of the cancerous tissue leaving only healthy skin cells.
  - If all the cancer is removed, then there is a good chance of recovery.
  - Surgery is typically used for skin, gastrointestinal, breast, uterus, cervix, prostate, and testicular cancer.

- **Radiation**
    - Process that alters the genetic material (cells) to prevent division, function, and, multiplication of the cancerous cells.
- **Chemotherapy**
    - Drugs are one of the more visible treatments because it causes hair loss.
    - Chemotherapy is a "drug cocktail" that destroys the ability to multiply, suppresses the immune system, and kills the bad cells.
    - This treatment typically is very hard on the patient.
- **Immunotherapy**
    - Group of drugs (**Interferon** is an example) triggers the immune system responses.
    - This treatment is also used for immune deficient diseases such as AIDS.
- **Alternative therapies**
    - Include acupressure, acupuncture, herbs, and diets
    - The results of alternative therapies have not been clinically proved to be effective for cancer.

Diabetes, arthritis, and genetic-related disorders

There are hundreds of genetic diseases and disorders. This guide will capture the ones most likely in an introductory health class.

Diabetes

Diabetes is a disease where the pancreas does not produce insulin, as it should. Insulin is used to process sugar and is a necessary component to body function. There are three types of diabetes:

- **Type 1**
    - Usually occurs during childhood and the person will spend a lifetime dependent on insulin injections.
    - A combination of monitoring the blood sugar level through blood samples and insulin injections makes the afflicted person responsible for working, as a pancreas should.

- **Type II (Diabetes mellitus)**
    - Type II diabetes is typically adult onset (obesity is a high risk factor).

- **Gestational diabetes**
    - Temporary condition that can happen to a woman during pregnancy.
    - After the baby is delivered blood sugar levels typically return to normal.

Asthma

There are several different types of asthma. The different types of asthma are:

- **Allergy**
    - Caused by allergic rhinitis (hay fever).
    - Inflammation of the lining inside the nose and is the most common asthma.

- o   Symptoms include; sneezing, running nose, and a cough.
- **Exercise-induced**
    - o   Triggered by physical exertion.
    - o   Some people without asthma develop asthma like symptoms during exercise.
    - o   Treatment includes pre-medication with an asthma inhaler before exercise.
- **Cough-variant**
    - o   The predominant symptom is severe coughing.
- **Occupational**
    - o   Triggered by the workplace.
    - o   Common workplaces susceptible to this asthma are animal breeders, farmers, hairdressers, nurses, and painters.
- **Nocturnal**
    - o   Symptoms happen at night and it can be very dangerous.
    - o   It may be caused from the increased exposure to allergens (indoor air is typically the dirtiest) and the reclining position.

ARTHRITIS
- **Rheumatoid arthritis**
    - o   An auto-immune response where the immune system attacks good joint tissue in all of the joints.
    - o   Symptoms of this disorder are stiffness, joint pain, swelling, redness, throbbing, muscle atrophy, joint deformity (fingers begin to curl), and limited mobility.

- **Osteoarthritis**
    - One name for over one hundred different conditions.
    - Osteoarthritis is caused by "wear and tear" on the joints (especially weight bearing ones, such as the hips and knees).
    - There is no cure; therefore treatment is comprised of pain management and/or joint replacement (depending on the severity).

GENETIC DISORDERS

Genetic disorders are diseases that are inherited from biological parents. Some of the common disorders that may appear on the test are:

- **Rett syndrome**
    - Severe genetic disorder affecting brain development.
    - It is almost exclusively found in girls with symptoms similar to autism.
    - Development slows after about 18 months, and children begin losing motor function.
    - There is no cure for Rett Syndrome.

- **Hemophilia**
    - Genetic disorder usually passed to sons from mothers with no symptoms.
    - A missing protein that is needed for blood clotting causes it.
    - Hemophiliacs are at risk for severe bleeding, internal bleeding, and surgery recovery.

- **Retinitis pitmentosa**
    - Hereditary eye disease that causes light sensitivity and the retina slowly degenerates into blindness.

- **Color blindness**
    - Hereditary condition that affects the ability to discern color.
    - While total color blindness (**monochromasy**) is rare, partial color blindness is common.
- **Cystic fibrosis**
    - Hereditary and fatal condition caused by a defective gene that causes the body to produce sticky mucus.
    - Due to medical advances, people with this condition can now live into their 40s.
- **Thalassemias**
    - Inherited blood disorders.
    - Thalassemias cause the body to make less hemoglobin (red blood cells rich in iron).
    - Anemia is caused by an iron deficiency.
- **Huntington's disease**
    - Genetically programmed degeneration of brain cells (neurons) in certain parts of the brain.
    - The degeneration causes loss of intellect, emotional disturbance, and uncontrolled movements.
    - A child of a Huntington's disease parent has a 50/50 chance of developing the disease.
    - If the gene is inherited, then the person will eventually develop the disease.
    - If the gene is not inherited, then the person cannot pass it to their subsequent children.

- **Polydactyly**
    - Condition where a child is born with extra toes or fingers.
    - This is a genetic disorder that is usually corrected by surgery during early childhood.
- **Achondroplasia**
    - Previously called dwarfism is an inherited condition.
- **Adult polycystic kidney disease**
    - Hereditary kidney disorder that has two forms.
        - It can manifest in adulthood or infancy.
        - In this disease the kidney has fluid filled growths (**cysts**) that impact the kidney functioning.

PART VI. CONSUMER AWARENESS, SAFETY, AND ENVIRONMENTAL CONCERNS

The consumer awareness, safety, and environmental concern component make up fifteen percent of the test.

CONSUMER AWARENESS

- Where do people typically find out information on health related issues?
    o Family and friends
    o Advertisements
    o Commercials
    o Folklore
    o Testimonials
    o Mass-media
    o Medical practitioner referrals
    o Health reference publications
    o Libraries
    o Advocacy groups
    o Government agencies
- Who are health care providers?
    o Physicians
    o Alternative care (chiropractors, acupuncturists, reflexology)
    o Restricted health care providers (dentists, nurses)
    o Allied health care professionals (operating room technicians, respiratory and inhalation therapists)

- What is the real difference between generic and brand name medication?
    - When a new drug is patented, the patent is good for 17 years.
    - After the 17 year patent expires drug companies can sell the same chemical formula and market under the generic name.
- Why are generics less expensive?
    - Generics are less expensive because there is a lot of money invested in research and development (R&D) and FDA approval.
    - The brand name has already done all of the costly work, so generics just need to replicate the patented formula.
    - Most of the time a generic can be substituted for a brand name, but there have been some concerns with the **bioavailability** (speed and extent drug is active in the body).
- Generic healthcare terms:
    - **Deductible amount**
        - Amount that the insured needs to pay before the insurance company pays.
    - **Fixed indemnity**
        - A benefit that lays out a specific amount for a procedure paid by the insurance company.
    - **Co-insurance**
        - Insurance company and patient share in the cost of covered services.
    - **Exclusion**
        - Items/procedures not covered in the policy

- **Health Maintenance Organization (HMO)**
    - A type of insurance where it advantage is cost containment.
    - Primary provider must be seen to obtain a referral to a specialist.
- **Preferred Provider Organization (PPO)**
    - A group of doctors who offer prepaid services out of their own offices (not in a central HMO office).
- **Government Insurance plans Medicare**
    - **Medicare**
        - Persons 65 and over that paid into the system receive medical benefits.
    - **Medicaid**
        - A medical benefit paid on a financial need basis.
- **Medicare supplement (Medigap)**
    - Insurance to cover the gap between what the Medicare insurance covers and the deductible and co-pays.

SAFETY CONCERNS

There are several types of safety concerns:

- **Personal safety**
    - Concerned with self-protection from harm.
    - Some common principles are to not assume safety, to think carefully, be aware of the surroundings, and avoid typical patterns.
    - Do not return home if being followed; go to a safe public place (such as a police department).

- **Residential safety**
    - Concerned with making the home a safe place to live.
    - Some common principles are to have:
        - A fire escape plan
        - Peep hole
        - Change locks when moving
        - Lock windows
        - Ask strangers (such as repair persons) to show their identification

- **Recreational safety**
    - Includes:
        - Wearing a seatbelt
        - Being cognizant of alcohol use
        - Learning to swim
        - Obeying laws

- **Firearm safety**
    - Includes:
        - Knowing gun possession laws in the state
        - Keeping firearms in good mechanical order
        - Never pointing a gun at an unintended target
        - Keeping your finger off the trigger
        - Educating children
        - Keeping it locked up
- **Motor vehicle safety**
    - Includes:
        - Keeping vehicle in good mechanical order
        - Wearing seatbelts
        - Not drinking and driving
        - Keeping noise at a reasonable level
        - Driving defensively
        - Giving pedestrians the right of way
- **Home accident**
    - Includes:
        - Adequate insurance
        - Keeping smoke detectors in working order
        - Child "proofing" a house with small children

ENVIRONMENTAL CONCERNS

Some of the gases in that are damaging our atmosphere are:

- Carbon dioxide
- Carbon monoxide
- Chlorofluorocarbons (CFCs)
- Methane
- Nitrous oxide

The **greenhouse effect** is when the solar heat is trapped in the atmosphere causing the Earth's surface to warm. This condition causes:

- Droughts
- Ice melting
- Acid rain
    - High pressure polluted air settles over an area creating an inversion layer.
    - The rain that is released is has a different pH level.
- Smog

Pollutant pathogens can be bacterial, viral, or protozoan. There are variety of ways water can become polluted:

- Animal waste
    - The bacteria **coliform** is an indicator of feces in the water.
- Biological imbalance
    - While a biological imbalance may be caused by aquatic plants that thrive in nitrate and phosphates used in fertilizers and detergents.

- Other toxins
- Toxins such as mercury and pesticides (DDT) that have mutagenic (mutations), **carcinogenic** (cancer), or **teratogenic** (birth defects) affects can make water unusable.

Land pollution is another environmental concern. Land pollution is caused by landfills that release chemicals into the land and, pesticides that are sprayed on plants cause land pollution. Other items that contribute to land pollution are:

- Nuclear reactors
- Accidents
- Radon gas

PRACTICE TEST

All test questions are in a multiple-choice format, with one correct answer and three incorrect options.

1. Which of the following is NOT a component of physical fitness?
    a. Muscular strength
    b. Flexibility
    c. Body composition
    d. They are ALL components of physical fitness

2. What is carboxyhemoglobin?
    a. When carbohydrates infuse into the blood
    b. When carbon monoxide in introduced into the blood stream
    c. When carbon dioxide molecules combine with red blood cells
    d. When carbon dioxide causes a bloody nose

3. Holistic health takes the following into consideration:
    a. Spiritual health
    b. Physical health
    c. Emotional health
    d. All of the above

4. Which kind of psychological disorder is categorized as "affective"?
    a. Bipolar disorder
    b. Anxiety
    c. Schizophrenia
    d. None of the above

5. The intoxicating ingredient in beer and wine is?
    a. Methanol
    b. Ispopropanol
    c. Butanol
    d. Ethanol

6. Which one of the below is NOT a controllable risk factor for heart disease?
    a. Smoking
    b. Physical activity
    c. Heredity
    d. Hypertension

7. What of the below is a good example of a remediation technique in the elderly?
    a. Physical therapy to learn to walk again after a fall
    b. Giving someone a scooter who's been afflicted with severe arthritis
    c. Teaching the elderly to read with one on one instruction
    d. None of the above

8. Drugs derived from opium are?
    a. Narcotic analgesics
    b. Hallucinogens
    c. Sedatives
    d. Tranquilizers

9. How many pints of blood does the average adult have?
    a. 2
    b. 10
    c. 6
    d. 9

10. What term is used for the people that reach the highest level of Maslow's hierarchy of need?
    a. Overachievers
    b. Winners
    c. Type A
    d. Transcenders

11. Which eating disorder is a psychological disorder when the sufferer abstains from food to unhealthy levels?
    a. Bulimia
    b. Anorexia
    c. Dieting
    d. None of the above

12. The primary stage of Dr. Hans Selye's general adaptation syndrome during which the body prepares to fight or flee is known as:
    a. Resistance
    b. Alarm
    c. Exhaustion
    d. Compulsion

13. When muscle elongates the action is called?
    a. Concentric
    b. Eccentric
    c. Isometric
    d. Ballistic

14. What is a good example of synethesia?
    a. Being able to describe the smell of a flower
    b. To evaluate a poem
    c. To taste a picture
    d. To identify a synthetic element

15. What condition forms white patches (usually from tobacco use) that are not easily removed on the tongue?
    a. Scar tissue
    b. Leukoplakia
    c. Swollen lymph nodes
    d. Mononucleosis

16. What kind of disorder is the sudden and medically unexplained loss of a body part?
    a. Anxiety disorder
    b. Affective disorder
    c. Somatoform disorder
    d. Anorexia Nervosa

17. What type of stress is defined by Dr. Selye as "good stress"?
    a. Eustress
    b. Distress
    c. Astress
    d. None of the above

18. Which of the following is NOT a part of the skeletal system?
    a. Tendons
    b. Ligaments
    c. Bone
    d. They are all a part of the skeletal system

19. What nutrients are calorie sources for your body?
    a. Protein
    b. Carbohydrates
    c. Fats
    d. All of the above

20. Fat soluble vitamins are:
    a. A, D, E, and K
    b. C, D, B, and A
    c. Calcium and Iron
    d. None of the above

21. Which of the following is a barrier form of birth control?
    a. The birth control pill
    b. Intrauterine device
    c. Diaphragm
    d. Rhythm method

22. What is the ABCD of getting mole checked out?
    a. Abnormal, blending, color, depth
    b. Asymmetric, border, color, diameter
    c. Abnormal, big, crescent, diameter
    d. Asymmetric, big, color, depth

23. What are the forms of fiber?
    a. Organic and inorganic
    b. Mineral and vitamin
    c. Plant derived and animal derived
    d. Soluble and insoluble

24. The type of immunity that develops from a vaccination is:
    a. Naturally acquired immunity (NAI)
    b. Artificially acquired immunity (AAI)
    c. Passively acquired immunity (PAI)
    d. Substitution acquired immunity (SAI)

25. The first major body system to develop is:
    a. Circulatory system
    b. Skeletal system
    c. Lymphatic system
    d. Digestive system

26. What is cortisol?
    a. A hormone significant in puberty
    b. A hormone that responds to stress
    c. A hormone that stimulates ovarian egg release
    d. Not a hormone at all

27. Which of the following is NOT a periodic abstinence form of birth control?
    a. Basal body temperature
    b. Billings cervical mucus
    c. Calendar
    d. Annual review method

28. What kind of vegetarian still consumes dairy products but no other animal by products?
    a. Vegan vegetarian
    b. Ovolactovegetarian
    c. Lactovegetarian
    d. None of the above

29. Hardening of the arteries is called:
    a. Arteritis
    b. Arteriosclerosis
    c. Atherosclerosis
    d. Angina pectoris

30. What does HIV stand for?
    a. Habitual Immune Virus
    b. Human Immune Virus
    c. Holistic Immunodeficiency Virus
    d. Human Immunodeficiency Virus

31. Which type of depression is best treated by medication?
    a. Secondary depression
    b. Adult onset depression
    c. Primary depression
    d. Childhood depression

32. The heart and the network of blood vessels leading to and from it comprise the:
    a. Cardiovascular system
    b. Respiratory system
    c. Endocrine system
    d. Reproductive system

33. A disease causing agent is:
    a. Pathogen
    b. Antagonist
    c. Antibody
    d. Vaccination

34. _____ is the process of a single sperm inserted into a single egg outside the woman's body.
    a. Gamete Intrafallopian Transfer (GIFT)
    b. In vitro fertilization
    c. Intracytoplasmic sperm injection
    d. Artificial insemination

35. Which of the following abnormalities can be detected by from an amniocentesis?
    a. Tay-Sachs disease
    b. Phocomelia
    c. Diabetes
    d. Cleft palate

36. Which cancer develops in the connective tissue?
    a. Carcinoma
    b. Leukemia
    c. Sarcoma
    d. Melanoma

37. Kubler-Ross' five stages of grieving are:
    a. Denial, anger, bargaining, depression, and acceptance
    b. Denial, rage, pleading, grief, closure
    c. Anger, sadness, grief, closure, moving on
    d. Sadness, anger, compromise, crying, closure

38. What is the primary difference between barbiturates and tranquilizers?
    a. Barbiturates are used to cope during waking hours
    b. Tranquilizers are used to cope during waking hours
    c. Tranquilizers are designed to cause sleep
    d. Barbiturates are no longer used in medical practices

39. Which drugs are known as "downers"?
    a. Stimulants
    b. Designer drugs
    c. Depressants
    d. Methamphetamines

40. What type of asthma is common for animal breeders, farmers and nurses?
    a. Allergy asthma
    b. Exercise-induced asthma
    c. Nocturnal asthma
    d. Occupational asthma

41. Which type of psychological disorder is related to anxiety?
    a. Psychogenic fugue
    b. Phobias
    c. Depression
    d. Schizophrenia

42. Which aspect of health focuses on creativity?
    a. Intellectual
    b. Physical
    c. Emotional
    d. All of the above

43. What kind of drug dependence is most dangerous?
    a. Psychological
    b. Emotional
    c. Physical
    d. Co-Dependence

44. The most basic (lowest) level of Maslow's hierarchy of needs is?
    a. Self actualization
    b. Esteem
    c. Love
    d. Physiological

45. What are the three stages of addiction?
    a. Introduction, compulsion, and over use
    b. Exposure, compulsion, and loss of control
    c. Exposure, attitude adaption, and loss of control
    d. None of the above

ANSWER KEY

1. D. (Muscular strength, flexibility, and body composition are ALL aspects of physical fitness).
2. C. Carboxyhemoglobin is when carbon dioxide molecules combine with red blood cells.
3. D. Holistic health takes spiritual, physical, and emotional health into consideration.
4. A. Bipolar (previously known as Manic Depressive) is known as an affective disorder.
5. D. The intoxicating ingredient in beer and wine is ethanol.
6. C. Heredity is NOT a controllable risk factor for heart disease (you can't choose your parents!)
7. B. Remediation is to substitute a lost function with something else. If someone doesn't have mobility giving them a scooter is a good example of providing mobility.
8. A. Drugs derived from opium are narcotic analgesics
9. C. The average adult has 6 pints of blood
10. D. Transcenders are people that accomplish Maslow's Self-Actualization
11. B. Anorexia is when a person starves themselves.
12. B. Alarm is the stage when the body prepares for "flight or fight"
13. B. When muscle elongates the action is called Eccentric
14. C. To "taste a picture" would be a good example of synesthesia
15. B. Leukoplakia is a condition with white patches on the tongue
16. C. A somatoform disorder is identified by the unexplained loss of a body part
17. A. Eustress is identified as "good stress"
18. D. Tendons, ligaments, and bones are all part of the skeletal system.
19. D. Proteins, carbohydrates, and fats are ALL sources of calories
20. A. A, D, E, and K are all fat soluble vitamins

21. C. Diaphragm is a barrier for of birth control

22. B. The ABCD's of moles are asymmetric, border, color, and diameter

23. D. The two types of fiber or soluble and insoluble

24. B. A vaccination is an example of Artificially acquired immunity

25. A. The first major system to develop in the fetus is the circulatory system

26. B. Cortisol is a hormone that responds to stress

27. D. There is no such thing as an "annual review" method of birth control

28. C. The Lactovegetarian still consumes dairy products

29. B. Arteriosclerosis is the hardening of the arteries

30. D. HIV stands for Human Immunodeficiency Virus

31. C. Primary depression is best treated by medication

32. A. The cardiovascular system is the heart and vessel network

33. A. A pathogen is a disease causing agent

34. C. Intracytoplasmic sperm injection is the process of inserting a single sperm into an egg

35. A. Tay-Sachs disease can be detected by an amniocentesis

36. C. Sarcoma is the cancer that develops in the connective tissue

37. A. Kubler-Ross five stages of grief are; denial, anger, bargaining, depression, and acceptance

38. B. Tranquilizers are designed to help people cope during waking hours

39. C. Depressants are also known as downers

40. D. Occupational asthma is often experienced by specific professions

41. B. Phobias are an anxiety disorder

42. A. Intellectuality is related to creativity

43. C. Physical drug dependence is the most dangerous

44. D. The most basic of Maslow's needs are physiological

45. B. Exposure, compulsion, and loss of control are the stages of addiction

INDEX

acme. *See* infection, stages of

acute alcohol intoxication. *See* alcohol poisoning

acute rhinitis, 71

addiction, 18

   compulsion, 18

   exposure, 18

   loss of control, 18

Adult Children of Alcoholics (ACOA), 44

affective disorders, 14

agent. *See* disease, components of

AIDS, 75, 90

alcohol

   effects of, 40

   types of, 40

alcohol poisoning, 42

Alcoholics Anonymous, 43

aleveoli, 46

Alzheimer's disease, 35

amniocentesis, 26

anatomical donations, 37

androgyny, 28

anemia, 27, 94

antigens, 70

anxiety, 13, 49

arthritis, 92

asphyxiation, 42

asthma, 91

attraction, 32

barbiturates, 48, 53

   common types, 49

   medical uses, 48

b-cells, 70

bereavement. *See* death

bipolar disorder, 14

birth, 19, 23

   bloody show, 24

   dilation, 21, 23

   effacement, 23

   transition, 24

birth control, 19

   abortion, 21

   barrier methods, 19

   contraception, 19, 20, 47

contraceptive drugs, 20
contraceptive pill, 20
intrauterine device, 21
periodic abstinence, 20
spermicidal fluid, 20
sterilization, 20
withdrawal, 20
cancer, 88
    treatment of, 89
    types of, 88
cannabis, 50
carboxyhemoglobin, 46
carcinogenic, 102
celibacy, 28
cells, 78
chippers, 45
chlamydia, 75, 76
chronic fatigue syndrome, 73
cigarettes, 45, 46
    gaseous, 46
    particulate, 46
cilia, 46
cirrhosis, 43

cocaine, 48, 52
    coke, 48
    crack, 48
    freebase, 48
COLD (Chronic Obstructive lung Disease), 46
coliform, 101
combing drugs, 54
communication, 31
    listening, 31
    nonverbal, 31
    verbal, 31
consumer awareness, 96
convalescent. *See* infection, stages of
conversion disorder, 14
cortisol, 16
crystal meth, 48
cystic fibrosis, 26
death, 19, 36, 38
Delirium tremens (DT), 44
depressants, 52, 53
depression, 9, 11, 37, 38, 74
    primary, 11
    secondary, 12

designer drugs, 53

diabetes, 91

disease

   components of, 68

dissociative disorders, 13

distress, 16

dysthymic, 14

eating disorders

   anorexia nervosa, 60

   bulimia nervosa, 60

empowerment, 9

entry point. *See* disease, components of

eustress, 16

euthanasia, 36

   direct, 36

   passive, 36

exercise, 58

   aerobic, 58

   anaerobic, 58

exit point. *See* disease, components of

fertilitiy

   artificial insemination, 22

   gamete intrafallopian transfer, 23

   in vitro fertilization, 22

   intracytoplasmic sperm injection, 23

fertility, 19, 20, 22, 23, 82

fetal alcohol syndrome, 42

food groups, 63, 64

General Adaptation Syndrome

   alarm, 16

   stage of exhaustion, 17

   stage of resistance, 16

general adaption syndrome, 16

generalized anxiety disorder, 13

genetic disorders, 93

   achondroplasia, 95

   adult polycystic kidney disease, 95

   color blindness, 94

   cystic fibrosis, 94

   hemophilia, 93

   huntington's disease, 94

   polydactyly, 95

   retinitis pitmentosa, 93

   rett syndrome, 93

   thalassemias, 94

genetics, 59

gestational diabetes, 27, 91

gonorrhea, 76

grains
  types of, 64

greenhouse effect, 101

grief
  stages of, 36

group B strep, 27

habituation. *See* substance abuse, psychological dependence

hallucinogens, 49, 52
  common types, 49

health
  holistic, 9

healthcare terms, 97

healthy aging, 19, 34

helper t-cells., 70

herbal supplements, 55
  echinacea, 55
  ginkgo biloba, 55
  milk thistle, 56
  St. John's Wort, 56

herpes simplex, 76

hospice care, 36

human immunodeficiency virus (HIV), 75

human papilloma virus (HPV), 76

hypochondria, 14

ice. *See* crystal meth

immune system
  types of, 70

immunity
  types of, 71

incubation. *See* infection, stages of

infection
  stages of, 69

influenza, 71

inhalants, 51, 52

intimate relationships, 19, 31

killer t-cells, 70

Kubler-Ross, 36

leukoplakia, 45

loneliness, 12

love, 33
  attachment, 33
  attraction, 33
  companionate, 33
  lust, 33

passionate, 32

lyme disease, 74

marijuana. *See* cannabis

Maslow
    Abraham, 9, 10, 104

measles, 74

memory t-cells, 70

menopause, 34, 86

microphages, 70

midlife, 34

mononucleosis, 73, 76

Mothers Against Drunk Driving (MADD), 43

mumps, 74

muscle strength, 58

narcolepsy, 53

narcotics, 50
    types of, 50

Neonatal Intensive Care Unit, 25

nicotine, 45

nutrients, 61, 65

obesity, 59
    hypercellular, 59
    hypertropic, 59

set-point theory, 59

obsessive compulsive disorder, 13

organs, 78

osteoarthritis, 34

osteoporosis, 34

panic, 13

pathogen, 68, 69

peak. *See* infection, stages of

Personalities
    Type A, 17
    Type B, 17

phobia, 13

phototherapy, 12

physical fitness, 57

pneumonia, 72

pregnancy, 19, 21, 23, 26, 42, 43, 87, 91
    first trimester, 24
    second trimester, 25
    third trimester, 25

prodormal. *See* infection, stages of

proof, 40

psychoactive drugs, 52

psychogenic amnesia, 14

psychogenic fugue, 14

psychotropic drugs. *See* psychoactive drugs

pulmonary emphysema, 46

reactive depression. *See* depression, secondary

recovery. *See* infection, stages of

rehabilitation, 35

remediation, 35

reproduction, 19

reservoir. *See* disease, components of

safety, 99

schizophrenic disorders, 15
    catatonic, 15
    disorganized, 15
    paranoid, 15

season affective disorder, 12

Selye, Hans, 16

sexuality, 19, 28
    bisexual, 29
    exhibitionism, 30
    fetishism, 29
    heterosexual, 29
    homosexual, 29
    masochism, 30
    psychosocial, 28
    sadism, 30
    sadomasochism, 30
    sexually deviant behaviors, 30
    transexual, 29
    transvestite, 29
    voyerism, 30

somatoform disorders, 14

spina bifida, 26

stressor, 16, 17

Students Against Drunk Driving (SADD), 43

substance abuse
    cross tolerance, 38
    physical dependence, 38
    psychological dependence, 38
    tolerance, 38

substance misuse, 39

suppressor t-cells, 70

syphilis
    stages of, 77

systems, 78
    cardiovascular, 82

digestive, 84
endocrine, 80
lymphatic, 83
muscular, 79
nervous, 79
reproductive, 86
respiratory, 83
skeletal, 78
urinary, 85
target heart rate, 57

tay-sachs, 26
teratogenic, 102
Theory Z, 10
tissues, 78
tranquilizers, 49, 53
   common types, 49
transcenders, 10
tuberculosis, 72
wills, 37

Made in the USA
San Bernardino, CA
31 October 2013